Freshwater Fish Tank Log Book

Maintenance Parameters
Date: / /

Temperature:	% Water Change:
pH Levels:	Ammonia Levels:
Nitrite Levels:	Nitrate Levels:
Alkalinity Levels:	Salinity Levels:
Phosphate Levels:	Added Water Conditioner: Y or N
Lights Schedule Time	**Feeding Schedule Times**
ON _____ AM	☐ _____ AM
OFF _____ PM	☐ _____ PM
Other:	Other:

General Observation Notes:

_____
_____
_____
_____
_____
_____

Freshwater Fish Tank Log Book

Maintenance Parameters
Date: / /

Temperature:	% Water Change:
pH Levels:	Ammonia Levels:
Nitrite Levels:	Nitrate Levels:
Alkalinity Levels:	Salinity Levels:
Phosphate Levels:	Added Water Conditioner: Y or N
Lights Schedule Time	**Feeding Schedule Times**
ON _____ AM	☐ _____ AM
OFF _____ PM	☐ _____ PM
Other:	Other:

General Observation Notes:

_____
_____
_____
_____
_____

Freshwater Fish Tank Log Book

Maintenance Parameters
Date: / /

Temperature:	% Water Change:
pH Levels:	Ammonia Levels:
Nitrite Levels:	Nitrate Levels:
Alkalinity Levels:	Salinity Levels:
Phosphate Levels:	Added Water Conditioner: Y or N
Lights Schedule Time	**Feeding Schedule Times**
ON _____ AM	☐ _____ AM
OFF _____ PM	☐ _____ PM
Other:	Other:

General Observation Notes:

_____

_____

_____

_____

_____

Freshwater Fish Tank Log Book

Maintenance Parameters
Date: / /

Temperature:	% Water Change:
pH Levels:	Ammonia Levels:
Nitrite Levels:	Nitrate Levels:
Alkalinity Levels:	Salinity Levels:
Phosphate Levels:	Added Water Conditioner: Y or N
Lights Schedule Time	**Feeding Schedule Times**
ON _____ AM	☐ _____ AM
OFF _____ PM	☐ _____ PM
Other:	Other:

General Observation Notes:

_____
_____
_____
_____
_____
_____

Freshwater Fish Tank Log Book

Maintenance Parameters
Date: / /

Temperature:	% Water Change:
pH Levels:	Ammonia Levels:
Nitrite Levels:	Nitrate Levels:
Alkalinity Levels:	Salinity Levels:
Phosphate Levels:	Added Water Conditioner: Y or N
Lights Schedule Time	**Feeding Schedule Times**
ON _____ AM	☐ _____ AM
OFF _____ PM	☐ _____ PM
Other:	Other:

General Observation Notes:

_____
_____
_____
_____
_____
_____

Freshwater Fish Tank Log Book

Maintenance Parameters
Date: / /

Temperature:	% Water Change:
pH Levels:	Ammonia Levels:
Nitrite Levels:	Nitrate Levels:
Alkalinity Levels:	Salinity Levels:
Phosphate Levels:	Added Water Conditioner: Y or N
Lights Schedule Time	**Feeding Schedule Times**
ON _____ AM	☐ _____ AM
OFF _____ PM	☐ _____ PM
Other:	Other:

General Observation Notes:

_____
_____
_____
_____
_____
_____

Freshwater Fish Tank Log Book

Maintenance Parameters
Date: / /

Temperature:	% Water Change:
pH Levels:	Ammonia Levels:
Nitrite Levels:	Nitrate Levels:
Alkalinity Levels:	Salinity Levels:
Phosphate Levels:	Added Water Conditioner: Y or N
Lights Schedule Time	**Feeding Schedule Times**
ON _____ AM	☐ _____ AM
OFF _____ PM	☐ _____ PM
Other:	Other:

General Observation Notes:

_____
_____
_____
_____
_____
_____
_____

Freshwater Fish Tank Log Book

Maintenance Parameters
Date: / /

Temperature:	% Water Change:
pH Levels:	Ammonia Levels:
Nitrite Levels:	Nitrate Levels:
Alkalinity Levels:	Salinity Levels:
Phosphate Levels:	Added Water Conditioner: Y or N
Lights Schedule Time	**Feeding Schedule Times**
ON _____ AM	☐ _____ AM
OFF _____ PM	☐ _____ PM
Other:	Other:

General Observation Notes:

_____
_____
_____
_____
_____
_____

Freshwater Fish Tank Log Book

Maintenance Parameters Date: / /	
Temperature:	% Water Change:
pH Levels:	Ammonia Levels:
Nitrite Levels:	Nitrate Levels:
Alkalinity Levels:	Salinity Levels:
Phosphate Levels:	Added Water Conditioner: Y or N
Lights Schedule Time	**Feeding Schedule Times**
ON _____ AM	☐ _____ AM
OFF _____ PM	☐ _____ PM
Other:	Other:

General Observation Notes:

_____

_____

_____

_____

_____

Freshwater Fish Tank Log Book

Maintenance Parameters
Date: / /

Temperature:	% Water Change:
pH Levels:	Ammonia Levels:
Nitrite Levels:	Nitrate Levels:
Alkalinity Levels:	Salinity Levels:
Phosphate Levels:	Added Water Conditioner: Y or N
Lights Schedule Time	**Feeding Schedule Times**
ON _____ AM	☐ _____ AM
OFF _____ PM	☐ _____ PM
Other:	Other:

General Observation Notes:

_____
_____
_____
_____
_____
_____

Freshwater Fish Tank Log Book

Maintenance Parameters
Date: /   /

Temperature:	% Water Change:
pH Levels:	Ammonia Levels:
Nitrite Levels:	Nitrate Levels:
Alkalinity Levels:	Salinity Levels:
Phosphate Levels:	Added Water Conditioner: Y or N
Lights Schedule Time	**Feeding Schedule Times**
ON _____ AM	☐ _____ AM
OFF _____ PM	☐ _____ PM
Other:	Other:

General Observation Notes:

_____
_____
_____
_____
_____
_____

Freshwater Fish Tank Log Book

Maintenance Parameters
Date: / /

Temperature:	% Water Change:
pH Levels:	Ammonia Levels:
Nitrite Levels:	Nitrate Levels:
Alkalinity Levels:	Salinity Levels:
Phosphate Levels:	Added Water Conditioner: Y or N
Lights Schedule Time	**Feeding Schedule Times**
ON _____ AM	☐ _____ AM
OFF _____ PM	☐ _____ PM
Other:	Other:

General Observation Notes:

Freshwater Fish Tank Log Book

Maintenance Parameters
Date: / /

Temperature:	% Water Change:
pH Levels:	Ammonia Levels:
Nitrite Levels:	Nitrate Levels:
Alkalinity Levels:	Salinity Levels:
Phosphate Levels:	Added Water Conditioner: Y or N
Lights Schedule Time	**Feeding Schedule Times**
ON _____ AM	☐ _____ AM
OFF _____ PM	☐ _____ PM
Other:	Other:

General Observation Notes:

_____
_____
_____
_____
_____
_____
_____

Freshwater Fish Tank Log Book

Maintenance Parameters
Date: / /

Temperature:	% Water Change:
pH Levels:	Ammonia Levels:
Nitrite Levels:	Nitrate Levels:
Alkalinity Levels:	Salinity Levels:
Phosphate Levels:	Added Water Conditioner: Y or N
Lights Schedule Time	**Feeding Schedule Times**
ON _____ AM	☐ _____ AM
OFF _____ PM	☐ _____ PM
Other:	Other:

General Observation Notes:

_____

_____

_____

_____

_____

_____

Freshwater Fish Tank Log Book

Maintenance Parameters Date: / /	
Temperature:	% Water Change:
pH Levels:	Ammonia Levels:
Nitrite Levels:	Nitrate Levels:
Alkalinity Levels:	Salinity Levels:
Phosphate Levels:	Added Water Conditioner: Y or N
Lights Schedule Time	**Feeding Schedule Times**
ON _____ AM	☐ _____ AM
OFF _____ PM	☐ _____ PM
Other:	Other:

General Observation Notes:

_____
_____
_____
_____
_____
_____
_____

Freshwater Fish Tank Log Book

Maintenance Parameters
Date: / /

Temperature:	% Water Change:
pH Levels:	Ammonia Levels:
Nitrite Levels:	Nitrate Levels:
Alkalinity Levels:	Salinity Levels:
Phosphate Levels:	Added Water Conditioner: Y or N
Lights Schedule Time	**Feeding Schedule Times**
ON _____ AM	☐ _____ AM
OFF _____ PM	☐ _____ PM
Other:	Other:

General Observation Notes:
_____
_____
_____
_____
_____
_____

Freshwater Fish Tank Log Book

Maintenance Parameters
Date: / /

Temperature:	% Water Change:
pH Levels:	Ammonia Levels:
Nitrite Levels:	Nitrate Levels:
Alkalinity Levels:	Salinity Levels:
Phosphate Levels:	Added Water Conditioner: Y or N
Lights Schedule Time	**Feeding Schedule Times**
ON _____ AM	☐ _____ AM
OFF _____ PM	☐ _____ PM
Other:	Other:

General Observation Notes:

_____
_____
_____
_____
_____
_____
_____

Freshwater Fish Tank Log Book

Maintenance Parameters
Date: / /

Temperature:	% Water Change:
pH Levels:	Ammonia Levels:
Nitrite Levels:	Nitrate Levels:
Alkalinity Levels:	Salinity Levels:
Phosphate Levels:	Added Water Conditioner: Y or N
Lights Schedule Time	**Feeding Schedule Times**
ON _____ AM	☐ _____ AM
OFF _____ PM	☐ _____ PM
Other:	Other:

General Observation Notes:

_____
_____
_____
_____
_____
_____

Freshwater Fish Tank Log Book

Maintenance Parameters
Date: / /

Temperature:	% Water Change:
pH Levels:	Ammonia Levels:
Nitrite Levels:	Nitrate Levels:
Alkalinity Levels:	Salinity Levels:
Phosphate Levels:	Added Water Conditioner: Y or N
Lights Schedule Time	**Feeding Schedule Times**
ON _____ AM	☐ _____ AM
OFF _____ PM	☐ _____ PM
Other:	Other:

General Observation Notes:

_____

_____

_____

_____

_____

_____

_____

Freshwater Fish Tank Log Book

Maintenance Parameters
Date: / /

Temperature:	% Water Change:
pH Levels:	Ammonia Levels:
Nitrite Levels:	Nitrate Levels:
Alkalinity Levels:	Salinity Levels:
Phosphate Levels:	Added Water Conditioner: Y or N
Lights Schedule Time	**Feeding Schedule Times**
ON _____ AM	☐ _____ AM
OFF _____ PM	☐ _____ PM
Other:	Other:

General Observation Notes:

_____

_____

_____

_____

_____

_____

Freshwater Fish Tank Log Book

Maintenance Parameters
Date: / /

Temperature:	% Water Change:
pH Levels:	Ammonia Levels:
Nitrite Levels:	Nitrate Levels:
Alkalinity Levels:	Salinity Levels:
Phosphate Levels:	Added Water Conditioner: Y or N
Lights Schedule Time	**Feeding Schedule Times**
ON _____ AM	☐ _____ AM
OFF _____ PM	☐ _____ PM
Other:	Other:

General Observation Notes:

_____
_____
_____
_____
_____
_____

Freshwater Fish Tank Log Book

Maintenance Parameters
Date: / /

Temperature:	% Water Change:
pH Levels:	Ammonia Levels:
Nitrite Levels:	Nitrate Levels:
Alkalinity Levels:	Salinity Levels:
Phosphate Levels:	Added Water Conditioner: Y or N
Lights Schedule Time	**Feeding Schedule Times**
ON _____ AM	☐ _____ AM
OFF _____ PM	☐ _____ PM
Other:	Other:

General Observation Notes:

_____

_____

_____

_____

_____

Freshwater Fish Tank Log Book

Maintenance Parameters
Date: / /

Temperature:	% Water Change:
pH Levels:	Ammonia Levels:
Nitrite Levels:	Nitrate Levels:
Alkalinity Levels:	Salinity Levels:
Phosphate Levels:	Added Water Conditioner: Y or N
Lights Schedule Time	**Feeding Schedule Times**
ON _____ AM	☐ _____ AM
OFF _____ PM	☐ _____ PM
Other:	Other:

General Observation Notes:

_____
_____
_____
_____
_____
_____

Freshwater Fish Tank Log Book

Maintenance Parameters
Date: / /

Temperature:	% Water Change:
pH Levels:	Ammonia Levels:
Nitrite Levels:	Nitrate Levels:
Alkalinity Levels:	Salinity Levels:
Phosphate Levels:	Added Water Conditioner: Y or N
Lights Schedule Time	**Feeding Schedule Times**
ON _____ AM	☐ _____ AM
OFF _____ PM	☐ _____ PM
Other:	Other:

General Observation Notes:

_____
_____
_____
_____
_____

Freshwater Fish Tank Log Book

Maintenance Parameters
Date: / /

Temperature:	% Water Change:
pH Levels:	Ammonia Levels:
Nitrite Levels:	Nitrate Levels:
Alkalinity Levels:	Salinity Levels:
Phosphate Levels:	Added Water Conditioner: Y or N
Lights Schedule Time	**Feeding Schedule Times**
ON _____ AM	☐ _____ AM
OFF _____ PM	☐ _____ PM
Other:	Other:

General Observation Notes:

_____
_____
_____
_____
_____

Freshwater Fish Tank Log Book

Maintenance Parameters
Date: / /

Temperature:	% Water Change:
pH Levels:	Ammonia Levels:
Nitrite Levels:	Nitrate Levels:
Alkalinity Levels:	Salinity Levels:
Phosphate Levels:	Added Water Conditioner: Y or N
Lights Schedule Time	**Feeding Schedule Times**
ON _____ AM	☐ _____ AM
OFF _____ PM	☐ _____ PM
Other:	Other:

General Observation Notes:

_____

_____

_____

_____

_____

Freshwater Fish Tank Log Book

Maintenance Parameters
Date: / /

Temperature:	% Water Change:
pH Levels:	Ammonia Levels:
Nitrite Levels:	Nitrate Levels:
Alkalinity Levels:	Salinity Levels:
Phosphate Levels:	Added Water Conditioner: Y or N
Lights Schedule Time	**Feeding Schedule Times**
ON _____ AM	☐ _____ AM
OFF _____ PM	☐ _____ PM
Other:	Other:

General Observation Notes:

_____

_____

_____

_____

_____

_____

Freshwater Fish Tank Log Book

Maintenance Parameters
Date: / /

Temperature:	% Water Change:
pH Levels:	Ammonia Levels:
Nitrite Levels:	Nitrate Levels:
Alkalinity Levels:	Salinity Levels:
Phosphate Levels:	Added Water Conditioner: Y or N
Lights Schedule Time	**Feeding Schedule Times**
ON _____ AM	☐ _____ AM
OFF _____ PM	☐ _____ PM
Other:	Other:

General Observation Notes:

Freshwater Fish Tank Log Book

Maintenance Parameters
Date: / /

Temperature:	% Water Change:
pH Levels:	Ammonia Levels:
Nitrite Levels:	Nitrate Levels:
Alkalinity Levels:	Salinity Levels:
Phosphate Levels:	Added Water Conditioner: Y or N
Lights Schedule Time	**Feeding Schedule Times**
ON _____ AM	☐ _____ AM
OFF _____ PM	☐ _____ PM
Other:	Other:

General Observation Notes:

_____
_____
_____
_____
_____
_____

Freshwater Fish Tank Log Book

Maintenance Parameters
Date: / /

Temperature:	% Water Change:
pH Levels:	Ammonia Levels:
Nitrite Levels:	Nitrate Levels:
Alkalinity Levels:	Salinity Levels:
Phosphate Levels:	Added Water Conditioner: Y or N
Lights Schedule Time	**Feeding Schedule Times**
ON _____ AM	☐ _____ AM
OFF _____ PM	☐ _____ PM
Other:	Other:

General Observation Notes:

_____

_____

_____

_____

Freshwater Fish Tank Log Book

Maintenance Parameters
Date: / /

Temperature:	% Water Change:
pH Levels:	Ammonia Levels:
Nitrite Levels:	Nitrate Levels:
Alkalinity Levels:	Salinity Levels:
Phosphate Levels:	Added Water Conditioner: Y or N
Lights Schedule Time	**Feeding Schedule Times**
ON _____ AM	☐ _____ AM
OFF _____ PM	☐ _____ PM
Other:	Other:

General Observation Notes:

_____

_____

_____

_____

_____

_____

Freshwater Fish Tank Log Book

Maintenance Parameters
Date: / /

Temperature:	% Water Change:
pH Levels:	Ammonia Levels:
Nitrite Levels:	Nitrate Levels:
Alkalinity Levels:	Salinity Levels:
Phosphate Levels:	Added Water Conditioner: Y or N
Lights Schedule Time	**Feeding Schedule Times**
ON _____ AM	☐ _____ AM
OFF _____ PM	☐ _____ PM
Other:	Other:

General Observation Notes:

_____

_____

_____

_____

_____

Freshwater Fish Tank Log Book

Maintenance Parameters Date: / /	
Temperature:	% Water Change:
pH Levels:	Ammonia Levels:
Nitrite Levels:	Nitrate Levels:
Alkalinity Levels:	Salinity Levels:
Phosphate Levels:	Added Water Conditioner: Y or N
Lights Schedule Time	**Feeding Schedule Times**
ON _____ AM	☐ _____ AM
OFF _____ PM	☐ _____ PM
Other:	Other:

General Observation Notes:

_____

_____

_____

_____

_____

_____

Freshwater Fish Tank Log Book

Maintenance Parameters
Date: / /

Temperature:	% Water Change:
pH Levels:	Ammonia Levels:
Nitrite Levels:	Nitrate Levels:
Alkalinity Levels:	Salinity Levels:
Phosphate Levels:	Added Water Conditioner: Y or N
Lights Schedule Time	**Feeding Schedule Times**
ON _____ AM	☐ _____ AM
OFF _____ PM	☐ _____ PM
Other:	Other:

General Observation Notes:

_____

_____

_____

_____

_____

Freshwater Fish Tank Log Book

Maintenance Parameters
Date: / /

Temperature:	% Water Change:
pH Levels:	Ammonia Levels:
Nitrite Levels:	Nitrate Levels:
Alkalinity Levels:	Salinity Levels:
Phosphate Levels:	Added Water Conditioner: Y or N
Lights Schedule Time	**Feeding Schedule Times**
ON _____ AM	☐ _____ AM
OFF _____ PM	☐ _____ PM
Other:	Other:

General Observation Notes:

_____

_____

_____

_____

_____

_____

Freshwater Fish Tank Log Book

Maintenance Parameters
Date: / /

Temperature:	% Water Change:
pH Levels:	Ammonia Levels:
Nitrite Levels:	Nitrate Levels:
Alkalinity Levels:	Salinity Levels:
Phosphate Levels:	Added Water Conditioner: Y or N
Lights Schedule Time	**Feeding Schedule Times**
ON _____ AM	☐ _____ AM
OFF _____ PM	☐ _____ PM
Other:	Other:

General Observation Notes:

_____

_____

_____

_____

_____

Freshwater Fish Tank Log Book

Maintenance Parameters
Date: / /

Temperature:	% Water Change:
pH Levels:	Ammonia Levels:
Nitrite Levels:	Nitrate Levels:
Alkalinity Levels:	Salinity Levels:
Phosphate Levels:	Added Water Conditioner: Y or N
Lights Schedule Time	**Feeding Schedule Times**
ON _____ AM	☐ _____ AM
OFF _____ PM	☐ _____ PM
Other:	Other:

General Observation Notes:

_____

_____

_____

_____

_____

Freshwater Fish Tank Log Book

Maintenance Parameters
Date: / /

Temperature:	% Water Change:
pH Levels:	Ammonia Levels:
Nitrite Levels:	Nitrate Levels:
Alkalinity Levels:	Salinity Levels:
Phosphate Levels:	Added Water Conditioner: Y or N
Lights Schedule Time	**Feeding Schedule Times**
ON _____ AM	☐ _____ AM
OFF _____ PM	☐ _____ PM
Other:	Other:

General Observation Notes:

_____

_____

_____

_____

_____

Freshwater Fish Tank Log Book

Maintenance Parameters Date: / /	
Temperature:	% Water Change:
pH Levels:	Ammonia Levels:
Nitrite Levels:	Nitrate Levels:
Alkalinity Levels:	Salinity Levels:
Phosphate Levels:	Added Water Conditioner: Y or N
Lights Schedule Time	**Feeding Schedule Times**
ON _____ AM	☐ _____ AM
OFF _____ PM	☐ _____ PM
Other:	Other:

General Observation Notes:

_____

_____

_____

_____

_____

_____

Freshwater Fish Tank Log Book

Maintenance Parameters
Date: / /

Temperature:	% Water Change:
pH Levels:	Ammonia Levels:
Nitrite Levels:	Nitrate Levels:
Alkalinity Levels:	Salinity Levels:
Phosphate Levels:	Added Water Conditioner: Y or N
Lights Schedule Time	**Feeding Schedule Times**
ON _____ AM	☐ _____ AM
OFF _____ PM	☐ _____ PM
Other:	Other:

General Observation Notes:

_____

_____

_____

_____

_____

Freshwater Fish Tank Log Book

Maintenance Parameters
Date: / /

Temperature:	% Water Change:
pH Levels:	Ammonia Levels:
Nitrite Levels:	Nitrate Levels:
Alkalinity Levels:	Salinity Levels:
Phosphate Levels:	Added Water Conditioner: Y or N
Lights Schedule Time	**Feeding Schedule Times**
ON _____ AM	☐ _____ AM
OFF _____ PM	☐ _____ PM
Other:	Other:

General Observation Notes:

_____

_____

_____

_____

_____

_____

Freshwater Fish Tank Log Book

Maintenance Parameters Date: / /	
Temperature:	% Water Change:
pH Levels:	Ammonia Levels:
Nitrite Levels:	Nitrate Levels:
Alkalinity Levels:	Salinity Levels:
Phosphate Levels:	Added Water Conditioner: Y or N
Lights Schedule Time	**Feeding Schedule Times**
ON _____ AM	☐ _____ AM
OFF _____ PM	☐ _____ PM
Other:	Other:

General Observation Notes:

Freshwater Fish Tank Log Book

Maintenance Parameters
Date: / /

Temperature:	% Water Change:
pH Levels:	Ammonia Levels:
Nitrite Levels:	Nitrate Levels:
Alkalinity Levels:	Salinity Levels:
Phosphate Levels:	Added Water Conditioner: Y or N
Lights Schedule Time	**Feeding Schedule Times**
ON _____ AM	☐ _____ AM
OFF _____ PM	☐ _____ PM
Other:	Other:

General Observation Notes:

_____

_____

_____

_____

_____

_____

Freshwater Fish Tank Log Book

Maintenance Parameters
Date: / /

Temperature:	% Water Change:
pH Levels:	Ammonia Levels:
Nitrite Levels:	Nitrate Levels:
Alkalinity Levels:	Salinity Levels:
Phosphate Levels:	Added Water Conditioner: Y or N
Lights Schedule Time	**Feeding Schedule Times**
ON _____ AM	☐ _____ AM
OFF _____ PM	☐ _____ PM
Other:	Other:

General Observation Notes:

_____

_____

_____

_____

_____

Freshwater Fish Tank Log Book

Maintenance Parameters
Date: / /

Temperature:	% Water Change:
pH Levels:	Ammonia Levels:
Nitrite Levels:	Nitrate Levels:
Alkalinity Levels:	Salinity Levels:
Phosphate Levels:	Added Water Conditioner: Y or N
Lights Schedule Time	**Feeding Schedule Times**
ON _____ AM	☐ _____ AM
OFF _____ PM	☐ _____ PM
Other:	Other:

General Observation Notes:

_____

_____

_____

_____

_____

Freshwater Fish Tank Log Book

Maintenance Parameters
Date: / /

Temperature:	% Water Change:
pH Levels:	Ammonia Levels:
Nitrite Levels:	Nitrate Levels:
Alkalinity Levels:	Salinity Levels:
Phosphate Levels:	Added Water Conditioner: Y or N
Lights Schedule Time	**Feeding Schedule Times**
ON _____ AM	☐ _____ AM
OFF _____ PM	☐ _____ PM
Other:	Other:

General Observation Notes:

Freshwater Fish Tank Log Book

Maintenance Parameters
Date: / /

Temperature:	% Water Change:
pH Levels:	Ammonia Levels:
Nitrite Levels:	Nitrate Levels:
Alkalinity Levels:	Salinity Levels:
Phosphate Levels:	Added Water Conditioner: Y or N
Lights Schedule Time	**Feeding Schedule Times**
ON _____ AM	☐ _____ AM
OFF _____ PM	☐ _____ PM
Other:	Other:

General Observation Notes:

_____

_____

_____

_____

_____

_____

Freshwater Fish Tank Log Book

Maintenance Parameters
Date: / /

Temperature:	% Water Change:
pH Levels:	Ammonia Levels:
Nitrite Levels:	Nitrate Levels:
Alkalinity Levels:	Salinity Levels:
Phosphate Levels:	Added Water Conditioner: Y or N
Lights Schedule Time	**Feeding Schedule Times**
ON _____ AM	☐ _____ AM
OFF _____ PM	☐ _____ PM
Other:	Other:

General Observation Notes:

_____
_____
_____
_____
_____
_____

Freshwater Fish Tank Log Book

Maintenance Parameters
Date: / /

Temperature:	% Water Change:
pH Levels:	Ammonia Levels:
Nitrite Levels:	Nitrate Levels:
Alkalinity Levels:	Salinity Levels:
Phosphate Levels:	Added Water Conditioner: Y or N
Lights Schedule Time	**Feeding Schedule Times**
ON _____ AM	☐ _____ AM
OFF _____ PM	☐ _____ PM
Other:	Other:

General Observation Notes:

_____
_____
_____
_____
_____
_____

Freshwater Fish Tank Log Book

Maintenance Parameters
Date: / /

Temperature:	% Water Change:
pH Levels:	Ammonia Levels:
Nitrite Levels:	Nitrate Levels:
Alkalinity Levels:	Salinity Levels:
Phosphate Levels:	Added Water Conditioner: Y or N
Lights Schedule Time	**Feeding Schedule Times**
ON _____ AM	☐ _____ AM
OFF _____ PM	☐ _____ PM
Other:	Other:

General Observation Notes:

_____

_____

_____

_____

_____

Freshwater Fish Tank Log Book

Maintenance Parameters Date: / /	
Temperature:	% Water Change:
pH Levels:	Ammonia Levels:
Nitrite Levels:	Nitrate Levels:
Alkalinity Levels:	Salinity Levels:
Phosphate Levels:	Added Water Conditioner: Y or N
Lights Schedule Time	**Feeding Schedule Times**
ON ―――― AM	☐ ―――― AM
OFF ―――― PM	☐ ―――― PM
Other:	Other:

General Observation Notes:

_____
_____
_____
_____
_____

Freshwater Fish Tank Log Book

Maintenance Parameters
Date: / /

Temperature:	% Water Change:
pH Levels:	Ammonia Levels:
Nitrite Levels:	Nitrate Levels:
Alkalinity Levels:	Salinity Levels:
Phosphate Levels:	Added Water Conditioner: Y or N
Lights Schedule Time	**Feeding Schedule Times**
ON _____ AM	☐ _____ AM
OFF _____ PM	☐ _____ PM
Other:	Other:

General Observation Notes:

_____

_____

_____

_____

_____

Freshwater Fish Tank Log Book

Maintenance Parameters
Date: / /

Temperature:	% Water Change:
pH Levels:	Ammonia Levels:
Nitrite Levels:	Nitrate Levels:
Alkalinity Levels:	Salinity Levels:
Phosphate Levels:	Added Water Conditioner: Y or N
Lights Schedule Time	**Feeding Schedule Times**
ON _____ AM	☐ _____ AM
OFF _____ PM	☐ _____ PM
Other:	Other:

General Observation Notes:

_____

_____

_____

_____

_____

_____

Freshwater Fish Tank Log Book

Maintenance Parameters
Date: / /

Temperature:	% Water Change:
pH Levels:	Ammonia Levels:
Nitrite Levels:	Nitrate Levels:
Alkalinity Levels:	Salinity Levels:
Phosphate Levels:	Added Water Conditioner: Y or N
Lights Schedule Time	**Feeding Schedule Times**
ON _____ AM	☐ _____ AM
OFF _____ PM	☐ _____ PM
Other:	Other:

General Observation Notes:

Freshwater Fish Tank Log Book ⋈

Maintenance Parameters
Date: / /

Temperature:	% Water Change:
pH Levels:	Ammonia Levels:
Nitrite Levels:	Nitrate Levels:
Alkalinity Levels:	Salinity Levels:
Phosphate Levels:	Added Water Conditioner: Y or N
Lights Schedule Time	**Feeding Schedule Times**
ON _____ AM	☐ _____ AM
OFF _____ PM	☐ _____ PM
Other:	Other:

General Observation Notes:

_____
_____
_____
_____
_____
_____

Freshwater Fish Tank Log Book

Maintenance Parameters
Date: / /

Temperature:	% Water Change:
pH Levels:	Ammonia Levels:
Nitrite Levels:	Nitrate Levels:
Alkalinity Levels:	Salinity Levels:
Phosphate Levels:	Added Water Conditioner: Y or N
Lights Schedule Time	**Feeding Schedule Times**
ON _____ AM	☐ _____ AM
OFF _____ PM	☐ _____ PM
Other:	Other:

General Observation Notes:

_____

_____

_____

_____

_____

Freshwater Fish Tank Log Book

Maintenance Parameters
Date: / /

Temperature:	% Water Change:
pH Levels:	Ammonia Levels:
Nitrite Levels:	Nitrate Levels:
Alkalinity Levels:	Salinity Levels:
Phosphate Levels:	Added Water Conditioner: Y or N
Lights Schedule Time	**Feeding Schedule Times**
ON _____ AM	☐ _____ AM
OFF _____ PM	☐ _____ PM
Other:	Other:

General Observation Notes:

_____

_____

_____

_____

_____

_____

Freshwater Fish Tank Log Book

Maintenance Parameters Date: / /	
Temperature:	% Water Change:
pH Levels:	Ammonia Levels:
Nitrite Levels:	Nitrate Levels:
Alkalinity Levels:	Salinity Levels:
Phosphate Levels:	Added Water Conditioner: Y or N
Lights Schedule Time	**Feeding Schedule Times**
ON _____ AM	☐ _____ AM
OFF _____ PM	☐ _____ PM
Other:	Other:

General Observation Notes:

_____
_____
_____
_____
_____

Freshwater Fish Tank Log Book

Maintenance Parameters
Date: / /

Temperature:	% Water Change:
pH Levels:	Ammonia Levels:
Nitrite Levels:	Nitrate Levels:
Alkalinity Levels:	Salinity Levels:
Phosphate Levels:	Added Water Conditioner: Y or N
Lights Schedule Time	**Feeding Schedule Times**
ON _____ AM	☐ _____ AM
OFF _____ PM	☐ _____ PM
Other:	Other:

General Observation Notes:

_____
_____
_____
_____
_____
_____

Freshwater Fish Tank Log Book

Maintenance Parameters
Date: / /

Temperature:	% Water Change:
pH Levels:	Ammonia Levels:
Nitrite Levels:	Nitrate Levels:
Alkalinity Levels:	Salinity Levels:
Phosphate Levels:	Added Water Conditioner: Y or N
Lights Schedule Time	**Feeding Schedule Times**
ON _____ AM	☐ _____ AM
OFF _____ PM	☐ _____ PM
Other:	Other:

General Observation Notes:

_____

_____

_____

_____

_____

Freshwater Fish Tank Log Book

Maintenance Parameters
Date: /   /

Temperature:	% Water Change:
pH Levels:	Ammonia Levels:
Nitrite Levels:	Nitrate Levels:
Alkalinity Levels:	Salinity Levels:
Phosphate Levels:	Added Water Conditioner: Y or N
Lights Schedule Time	**Feeding Schedule Times**
ON _____ AM	☐ _____ AM
OFF _____ PM	☐ _____ PM
Other:	Other:

General Observation Notes:

_____

_____

_____

_____

_____

Freshwater Fish Tank Log Book

Maintenance Parameters
Date: / /

Temperature:	% Water Change:
pH Levels:	Ammonia Levels:
Nitrite Levels:	Nitrate Levels:
Alkalinity Levels:	Salinity Levels:
Phosphate Levels:	Added Water Conditioner: Y or N
Lights Schedule Time	**Feeding Schedule Times**
ON _____ AM	☐ _____ AM
OFF _____ PM	☐ _____ PM
Other:	Other:

General Observation Notes:

_____

_____

_____

_____

_____

Freshwater Fish Tank Log Book

Maintenance Parameters
Date: / /

Temperature:	% Water Change:
pH Levels:	Ammonia Levels:
Nitrite Levels:	Nitrate Levels:
Alkalinity Levels:	Salinity Levels:
Phosphate Levels:	Added Water Conditioner: Y or N
Lights Schedule Time	**Feeding Schedule Times**
ON _____ AM	☐ _____ AM
OFF _____ PM	☐ _____ PM
Other:	Other:

General Observation Notes:

_____
_____
_____
_____
_____
_____

Freshwater Fish Tank Log Book

Maintenance Parameters
Date: /   /

Temperature:	% Water Change:
pH Levels:	Ammonia Levels:
Nitrite Levels:	Nitrate Levels:
Alkalinity Levels:	Salinity Levels:
Phosphate Levels:	Added Water Conditioner: Y or N
Lights Schedule Time	**Feeding Schedule Times**
ON _____ AM	☐ _____ AM
OFF _____ PM	☐ _____ PM
Other:	Other:

General Observation Notes:

_____
_____
_____
_____
_____

Freshwater Fish Tank Log Book

Maintenance Parameters
Date: / /

Temperature:	% Water Change:
pH Levels:	Ammonia Levels:
Nitrite Levels:	Nitrate Levels:
Alkalinity Levels:	Salinity Levels:
Phosphate Levels:	Added Water Conditioner: Y or N
Lights Schedule Time	**Feeding Schedule Times**
ON _____ AM	☐ _____ AM
OFF _____ PM	☐ _____ PM
Other:	Other:

General Observation Notes:

_____

_____

_____

_____

_____

_____

Freshwater Fish Tank Log Book

Maintenance Parameters
Date: / /

Temperature:	% Water Change:
pH Levels:	Ammonia Levels:
Nitrite Levels:	Nitrate Levels:
Alkalinity Levels:	Salinity Levels:
Phosphate Levels:	Added Water Conditioner: Y or N
Lights Schedule Time	**Feeding Schedule Times**
ON _____ AM	☐ _____ AM
OFF _____ PM	☐ _____ PM
Other:	Other:

General Observation Notes:

_____

_____

_____

_____

_____

Freshwater Fish Tank Log Book

Maintenance Parameters
Date: / /

Temperature:	% Water Change:
pH Levels:	Ammonia Levels:
Nitrite Levels:	Nitrate Levels:
Alkalinity Levels:	Salinity Levels:
Phosphate Levels:	Added Water Conditioner: Y or N
Lights Schedule Time	**Feeding Schedule Times**
ON _____ AM	☐ _____ AM
OFF _____ PM	☐ _____ PM
Other:	Other:

General Observation Notes:

_____

_____

_____

_____

_____

Freshwater Fish Tank Log Book

Maintenance Parameters
Date: / /

Temperature:	% Water Change:
pH Levels:	Ammonia Levels:
Nitrite Levels:	Nitrate Levels:
Alkalinity Levels:	Salinity Levels:
Phosphate Levels:	Added Water Conditioner: Y or N
Lights Schedule Time	**Feeding Schedule Times**
ON _____ AM	☐ _____ AM
OFF _____ PM	☐ _____ PM
Other:	Other:

General Observation Notes:

_____

_____

_____

_____

_____

Freshwater Fish Tank Log Book

Maintenance Parameters Date: / /	
Temperature:	% Water Change:
pH Levels:	Ammonia Levels:
Nitrite Levels:	Nitrate Levels:
Alkalinity Levels:	Salinity Levels:
Phosphate Levels:	Added Water Conditioner: Y or N
Lights Schedule Time	**Feeding Schedule Times**
ON _____ AM	☐ _____ AM
OFF _____ PM	☐ _____ PM
Other:	Other:

General Observation Notes:

_____
_____
_____
_____
_____
_____

Freshwater Fish Tank Log Book

Maintenance Parameters
Date: / /

Temperature:	% Water Change:
pH Levels:	Ammonia Levels:
Nitrite Levels:	Nitrate Levels:
Alkalinity Levels:	Salinity Levels:
Phosphate Levels:	Added Water Conditioner: Y or N
Lights Schedule Time	**Feeding Schedule Times**
ON _____ AM	☐ _____ AM
OFF _____ PM	☐ _____ PM
Other:	Other:

General Observation Notes:

_____

_____

_____

_____

_____

Freshwater Fish Tank Log Book

Maintenance Parameters
Date: / /

Temperature:	% Water Change:
pH Levels:	Ammonia Levels:
Nitrite Levels:	Nitrate Levels:
Alkalinity Levels:	Salinity Levels:
Phosphate Levels:	Added Water Conditioner: Y or N
Lights Schedule Time	**Feeding Schedule Times**
ON _____ AM	☐ _____ AM
OFF _____ PM	☐ _____ PM
Other:	Other:

General Observation Notes:

_____
_____
_____
_____
_____
_____

Freshwater Fish Tank Log Book

Maintenance Parameters Date: / /	
Temperature:	% Water Change:
pH Levels:	Ammonia Levels:
Nitrite Levels:	Nitrate Levels:
Alkalinity Levels:	Salinity Levels:
Phosphate Levels:	Added Water Conditioner: Y or N
Lights Schedule Time	**Feeding Schedule Times**
ON _____ AM	☐ _____ AM
OFF _____ PM	☐ _____ PM
Other:	Other:

General Observation Notes:

Freshwater Fish Tank Log Book 🐟

Maintenance Parameters
Date: / /

Temperature:	% Water Change:
pH Levels:	Ammonia Levels:
Nitrite Levels:	Nitrate Levels:
Alkalinity Levels:	Salinity Levels:
Phosphate Levels:	Added Water Conditioner: Y or N
Lights Schedule Time	**Feeding Schedule Times**
ON _____ AM	☐ _____ AM
OFF _____ PM	☐ _____ PM
Other:	Other:

General Observation Notes:

Freshwater Fish Tank Log Book

Maintenance Parameters
Date: / /

Temperature:	% Water Change:
pH Levels:	Ammonia Levels:
Nitrite Levels:	Nitrate Levels:
Alkalinity Levels:	Salinity Levels:
Phosphate Levels:	Added Water Conditioner: Y or N
Lights Schedule Time	**Feeding Schedule Times**
ON _____ AM	☐ _____ AM
OFF _____ PM	☐ _____ PM
Other:	Other:

General Observation Notes:

_____
_____
_____
_____
_____

Freshwater Fish Tank Log Book

Maintenance Parameters
Date: / /

Temperature:	% Water Change:
pH Levels:	Ammonia Levels:
Nitrite Levels:	Nitrate Levels:
Alkalinity Levels:	Salinity Levels:
Phosphate Levels:	Added Water Conditioner: Y or N
Lights Schedule Time	**Feeding Schedule Times**
ON _____ AM	☐ _____ AM
OFF _____ PM	☐ _____ PM
Other:	Other:

General Observation Notes:

_____
_____
_____
_____
_____

Freshwater Fish Tank Log Book

Maintenance Parameters
Date: / /

Temperature:	% Water Change:
pH Levels:	Ammonia Levels:
Nitrite Levels:	Nitrate Levels:
Alkalinity Levels:	Salinity Levels:
Phosphate Levels:	Added Water Conditioner: Y or N
Lights Schedule Time	**Feeding Schedule Times**
ON _____ AM	☐ _____ AM
OFF _____ PM	☐ _____ PM
Other:	Other:

General Observation Notes:

_____

_____

_____

_____

_____

Freshwater Fish Tank Log Book

Maintenance Parameters
Date: / /

Temperature:	% Water Change:
pH Levels:	Ammonia Levels:
Nitrite Levels:	Nitrate Levels:
Alkalinity Levels:	Salinity Levels:
Phosphate Levels:	Added Water Conditioner: Y or N
Lights Schedule Time	**Feeding Schedule Times**
ON _____ AM	☐ _____ AM
OFF _____ PM	☐ _____ PM
Other:	Other:

General Observation Notes:

_____
_____
_____
_____
_____
_____

Freshwater Fish Tank Log Book

Maintenance Parameters
Date: / /

Temperature:	% Water Change:
pH Levels:	Ammonia Levels:
Nitrite Levels:	Nitrate Levels:
Alkalinity Levels:	Salinity Levels:
Phosphate Levels:	Added Water Conditioner: Y or N
Lights Schedule Time	**Feeding Schedule Times**
ON _____ AM	☐ _____ AM
OFF _____ PM	☐ _____ PM
Other:	Other:

General Observation Notes:

_____

_____

_____

_____

_____

_____

Freshwater Fish Tank Log Book

Maintenance Parameters
Date: / /

Temperature:	% Water Change:
pH Levels:	Ammonia Levels:
Nitrite Levels:	Nitrate Levels:
Alkalinity Levels:	Salinity Levels:
Phosphate Levels:	Added Water Conditioner: Y or N
Lights Schedule Time	**Feeding Schedule Times**
ON _____ AM	☐ _____ AM
OFF _____ PM	☐ _____ PM
Other:	Other:

General Observation Notes:
_____
_____
_____
_____
_____
_____

Freshwater Fish Tank Log Book

Maintenance Parameters
Date: / /

Temperature:	% Water Change:
pH Levels:	Ammonia Levels:
Nitrite Levels:	Nitrate Levels:
Alkalinity Levels:	Salinity Levels:
Phosphate Levels:	Added Water Conditioner: Y or N
Lights Schedule Time	**Feeding Schedule Times**
ON _____ AM	☐ _____ AM
OFF _____ PM	☐ _____ PM
Other:	Other:

General Observation Notes:

_____

_____

_____

_____

_____

Freshwater Fish Tank Log Book

Maintenance Parameters
Date: / /

Temperature:	% Water Change:
pH Levels:	Ammonia Levels:
Nitrite Levels:	Nitrate Levels:
Alkalinity Levels:	Salinity Levels:
Phosphate Levels:	Added Water Conditioner: Y or N
Lights Schedule Time	**Feeding Schedule Times**
ON _____ AM	☐ _____ AM
OFF _____ PM	☐ _____ PM
Other:	Other:

General Observation Notes:

_____

_____

_____

_____

_____

_____

Freshwater Fish Tank Log Book

Maintenance Parameters Date: / /	
Temperature:	% Water Change:
pH Levels:	Ammonia Levels:
Nitrite Levels:	Nitrate Levels:
Alkalinity Levels:	Salinity Levels:
Phosphate Levels:	Added Water Conditioner: Y or N
Lights Schedule Time	**Feeding Schedule Times**
ON _____ AM	☐ _____ AM
OFF _____ PM	☐ _____ PM
Other:	Other:

General Observation Notes:

Freshwater Fish Tank Log Book

Maintenance Parameters
Date: / /

Temperature:	% Water Change:
pH Levels:	Ammonia Levels:
Nitrite Levels:	Nitrate Levels:
Alkalinity Levels:	Salinity Levels:
Phosphate Levels:	Added Water Conditioner: Y or N
Lights Schedule Time	**Feeding Schedule Times**
ON _____ AM	☐ _____ AM
OFF _____ PM	☐ _____ PM
Other:	Other:

General Observation Notes:

_____
_____
_____
_____
_____
_____
_____

Freshwater Fish Tank Log Book

Maintenance Parameters
Date: / /

Temperature:	% Water Change:
pH Levels:	Ammonia Levels:
Nitrite Levels:	Nitrate Levels:
Alkalinity Levels:	Salinity Levels:
Phosphate Levels:	Added Water Conditioner: Y or N
Lights Schedule Time	**Feeding Schedule Times**
ON _____ AM	☐ _____ AM
OFF _____ PM	☐ _____ PM
Other:	Other:

General Observation Notes:

_____

_____

_____

_____

_____

_____

Freshwater Fish Tank Log Book 🐟

Maintenance Parameters
Date: / /

Temperature:	% Water Change:
pH Levels:	Ammonia Levels:
Nitrite Levels:	Nitrate Levels:
Alkalinity Levels:	Salinity Levels:
Phosphate Levels:	Added Water Conditioner: Y or N
Lights Schedule Time	**Feeding Schedule Times**
ON _____ AM	☐ _____ AM
OFF _____ PM	☐ _____ PM
Other:	Other:

General Observation Notes:

_____

_____

_____

_____

_____

_____

Freshwater Fish Tank Log Book 〉◇〈

Maintenance Parameters Date: / /	
Temperature:	% Water Change:
pH Levels:	Ammonia Levels:
Nitrite Levels:	Nitrate Levels:
Alkalinity Levels:	Salinity Levels:
Phosphate Levels:	Added Water Conditioner: Y or N
Lights Schedule Time	**Feeding Schedule Times**
ON _____ AM	☐ _____ AM
OFF _____ PM	☐ _____ PM
Other:	Other:

General Observation Notes:

_____
_____
_____
_____
_____

Freshwater Fish Tank Log Book

Maintenance Parameters
Date: / /

Temperature:	% Water Change:
pH Levels:	Ammonia Levels:
Nitrite Levels:	Nitrate Levels:
Alkalinity Levels:	Salinity Levels:
Phosphate Levels:	Added Water Conditioner: Y or N
Lights Schedule Time	**Feeding Schedule Times**
ON _____ AM	☐ _____ AM
OFF _____ PM	☐ _____ PM
Other:	Other:

General Observation Notes:

_____

_____

_____

_____

_____

Freshwater Fish Tank Log Book

Maintenance Parameters Date: / /	
Temperature:	% Water Change:
pH Levels:	Ammonia Levels:
Nitrite Levels:	Nitrate Levels:
Alkalinity Levels:	Salinity Levels:
Phosphate Levels:	Added Water Conditioner: Y or N
Lights Schedule Time	**Feeding Schedule Times**
ON _____ AM	☐ _____ AM
OFF _____ PM	☐ _____ PM
Other:	Other:

General Observation Notes:

_____
_____
_____
_____
_____
_____

Freshwater Fish Tank Log Book

Maintenance Parameters
Date: / /

Temperature:	% Water Change:
pH Levels:	Ammonia Levels:
Nitrite Levels:	Nitrate Levels:
Alkalinity Levels:	Salinity Levels:
Phosphate Levels:	Added Water Conditioner: Y or N
Lights Schedule Time	**Feeding Schedule Times**
ON _____ AM	☐ _____ AM
OFF _____ PM	☐ _____ PM
Other:	Other:

General Observation Notes:

_____

_____

_____

_____

_____

Freshwater Fish Tank Log Book

Maintenance Parameters
Date: / /

Temperature:	% Water Change:
pH Levels:	Ammonia Levels:
Nitrite Levels:	Nitrate Levels:
Alkalinity Levels:	Salinity Levels:
Phosphate Levels:	Added Water Conditioner: Y or N
Lights Schedule Time	**Feeding Schedule Times**
ON _____ AM	☐ _____ AM
OFF _____ PM	☐ _____ PM
Other:	Other:

General Observation Notes:

_____

Freshwater Fish Tank Log Book

Maintenance Parameters Date: / /	
Temperature:	% Water Change:
pH Levels:	Ammonia Levels:
Nitrite Levels:	Nitrate Levels:
Alkalinity Levels:	Salinity Levels:
Phosphate Levels:	Added Water Conditioner: Y or N
Lights Schedule Time	**Feeding Schedule Times**
ON _____ AM	☐ _____ AM
OFF _____ PM	☐ _____ PM
Other:	Other:

General Observation Notes:

_____
_____
_____
_____
_____

Freshwater Fish Tank Log Book

Maintenance Parameters
Date: / /

Temperature:	% Water Change:
pH Levels:	Ammonia Levels:
Nitrite Levels:	Nitrate Levels:
Alkalinity Levels:	Salinity Levels:
Phosphate Levels:	Added Water Conditioner: Y or N
Lights Schedule Time	**Feeding Schedule Times**
ON _____ AM	☐ _____ AM
OFF _____ PM	☐ _____ PM
Other:	Other:

General Observation Notes:

_____

_____

_____

_____

_____

Freshwater Fish Tank Log Book

Maintenance Parameters Date: / /	
Temperature:	% Water Change:
pH Levels:	Ammonia Levels:
Nitrite Levels:	Nitrate Levels:
Alkalinity Levels:	Salinity Levels:
Phosphate Levels:	Added Water Conditioner: Y or N
Lights Schedule Time	**Feeding Schedule Times**
ON _____ AM	☐ _____ AM
OFF _____ PM	☐ _____ PM
Other:	Other:

General Observation Notes:

_____
_____
_____
_____
_____
_____

Freshwater Fish Tank Log Book

Maintenance Parameters
Date: / /

Temperature:	% Water Change:
pH Levels:	Ammonia Levels:
Nitrite Levels:	Nitrate Levels:
Alkalinity Levels:	Salinity Levels:
Phosphate Levels:	Added Water Conditioner: Y or N
Lights Schedule Time	**Feeding Schedule Times**
ON _____ AM	☐ _____ AM
OFF _____ PM	☐ _____ PM
Other:	Other:

General Observation Notes:

_____

_____

_____

_____

_____

Freshwater Fish Tank Log Book

Maintenance Parameters
Date: / /

Temperature:	% Water Change:
pH Levels:	Ammonia Levels:
Nitrite Levels:	Nitrate Levels:
Alkalinity Levels:	Salinity Levels:
Phosphate Levels:	Added Water Conditioner: Y or N
Lights Schedule Time	**Feeding Schedule Times**
ON _____ AM	☐ _____ AM
OFF _____ PM	☐ _____ PM
Other:	Other:

General Observation Notes:

_____
_____
_____
_____
_____
_____

Freshwater Fish Tank Log Book

Maintenance Parameters
Date: / /

Temperature:	% Water Change:
pH Levels:	Ammonia Levels:
Nitrite Levels:	Nitrate Levels:
Alkalinity Levels:	Salinity Levels:
Phosphate Levels:	Added Water Conditioner: Y or N
Lights Schedule Time	**Feeding Schedule Times**
ON _____ AM	☐ _____ AM
OFF _____ PM	☐ _____ PM
Other:	Other:

General Observation Notes:

_____

_____

_____

_____

_____

_____

Freshwater Fish Tank Log Book

Maintenance Parameters
Date: / /

Temperature:	% Water Change:
pH Levels:	Ammonia Levels:
Nitrite Levels:	Nitrate Levels:
Alkalinity Levels:	Salinity Levels:
Phosphate Levels:	Added Water Conditioner: Y or N
Lights Schedule Time	**Feeding Schedule Times**
ON _____ AM	☐ _____ AM
OFF _____ PM	☐ _____ PM
Other:	Other:

General Observation Notes:

_____
_____
_____
_____
_____
_____

Freshwater Fish Tank Log Book

Maintenance Parameters
Date: / /

Temperature:	% Water Change:
pH Levels:	Ammonia Levels:
Nitrite Levels:	Nitrate Levels:
Alkalinity Levels:	Salinity Levels:
Phosphate Levels:	Added Water Conditioner: Y or N
Lights Schedule Time	**Feeding Schedule Times**
ON _____ AM	☐ _____ AM
OFF _____ PM	☐ _____ PM
Other:	Other:

General Observation Notes:

_____

_____

_____

_____

_____

Freshwater Fish Tank Log Book

Maintenance Parameters
Date: / /

Temperature:	% Water Change:
pH Levels:	Ammonia Levels:
Nitrite Levels:	Nitrate Levels:
Alkalinity Levels:	Salinity Levels:
Phosphate Levels:	Added Water Conditioner: Y or N
Lights Schedule Time	**Feeding Schedule Times**
ON _____ AM	☐ _____ AM
OFF _____ PM	☐ _____ PM
Other:	Other:

General Observation Notes:

_____
_____
_____
_____
_____
_____

Freshwater Fish Tank Log Book

Maintenance Parameters
Date: / /

Temperature:	% Water Change:
pH Levels:	Ammonia Levels:
Nitrite Levels:	Nitrate Levels:
Alkalinity Levels:	Salinity Levels:
Phosphate Levels:	Added Water Conditioner: Y or N
Lights Schedule Time	**Feeding Schedule Times**
ON _____ AM	☐ _____ AM
OFF _____ PM	☐ _____ PM
Other:	Other:

General Observation Notes:

_____

_____

_____

_____

_____

Freshwater Fish Tank Log Book

Maintenance Parameters
Date: / /

Temperature:	% Water Change:
pH Levels:	Ammonia Levels:
Nitrite Levels:	Nitrate Levels:
Alkalinity Levels:	Salinity Levels:
Phosphate Levels:	Added Water Conditioner: Y or N
Lights Schedule Time	**Feeding Schedule Times**
ON _____ AM	☐ _____ AM
OFF _____ PM	☐ _____ PM
Other:	Other:

General Observation Notes:

_____
_____
_____
_____
_____

Freshwater Fish Tank Log Book

Maintenance Parameters
Date: / /

Temperature:	% Water Change:
pH Levels:	Ammonia Levels:
Nitrite Levels:	Nitrate Levels:
Alkalinity Levels:	Salinity Levels:
Phosphate Levels:	Added Water Conditioner: Y or N
Lights Schedule Time	**Feeding Schedule Times**
ON _____ AM	☐ _____ AM
OFF _____ PM	☐ _____ PM
Other:	Other:

General Observation Notes:

_____
_____
_____
_____
_____

Freshwater Fish Tank Log Book ><

Maintenance Parameters
Date: / /

Temperature:	% Water Change:
pH Levels:	Ammonia Levels:
Nitrite Levels:	Nitrate Levels:
Alkalinity Levels:	Salinity Levels:
Phosphate Levels:	Added Water Conditioner: Y or N
Lights Schedule Time	**Feeding Schedule Times**
ON _____ AM	☐ _____ AM
OFF _____ PM	☐ _____ PM
Other:	Other:

General Observation Notes:

_____
_____
_____
_____
_____
_____

Freshwater Fish Tank Log Book ><><

Maintenance Parameters
Date: / /

Temperature:	% Water Change:
pH Levels:	Ammonia Levels:
Nitrite Levels:	Nitrate Levels:
Alkalinity Levels:	Salinity Levels:
Phosphate Levels:	Added Water Conditioner: Y or N
Lights Schedule Time	**Feeding Schedule Times**
ON _____ AM	☐ _____ AM
OFF _____ PM	☐ _____ PM
Other:	Other:

General Observation Notes:

_____

_____

_____

_____

_____

Freshwater Fish Tank Log Book

Maintenance Parameters
Date: / /

Temperature:	% Water Change:
pH Levels:	Ammonia Levels:
Nitrite Levels:	Nitrate Levels:
Alkalinity Levels:	Salinity Levels:
Phosphate Levels:	Added Water Conditioner: Y or N
Lights Schedule Time	**Feeding Schedule Times**
ON _____ AM	☐ _____ AM
OFF _____ PM	☐ _____ PM
Other:	Other:

General Observation Notes:

_____
_____
_____
_____
_____
_____
_____

Freshwater Fish Tank Log Book

Maintenance Parameters
Date: / /

Temperature:	% Water Change:
pH Levels:	Ammonia Levels:
Nitrite Levels:	Nitrate Levels:
Alkalinity Levels:	Salinity Levels:
Phosphate Levels:	Added Water Conditioner: Y or N
Lights Schedule Time	**Feeding Schedule Times**
ON _____ AM	☐ _____ AM
OFF _____ PM	☐ _____ PM
Other:	Other:

General Observation Notes:

_____

_____

_____

_____

_____

Freshwater Fish Tank Log Book

Maintenance Parameters
Date: / /

Temperature:	% Water Change:
pH Levels:	Ammonia Levels:
Nitrite Levels:	Nitrate Levels:
Alkalinity Levels:	Salinity Levels:
Phosphate Levels:	Added Water Conditioner: Y or N
Lights Schedule Time	**Feeding Schedule Times**
ON _____ AM	☐ _____ AM
OFF _____ PM	☐ _____ PM
Other:	Other:

General Observation Notes:

_____
_____
_____
_____
_____
_____

Freshwater Fish Tank Log Book

Maintenance Parameters
Date: / /

Temperature:	% Water Change:
pH Levels:	Ammonia Levels:
Nitrite Levels:	Nitrate Levels:
Alkalinity Levels:	Salinity Levels:
Phosphate Levels:	Added Water Conditioner: Y or N
Lights Schedule Time	**Feeding Schedule Times**
ON _____ AM	☐ _____ AM
OFF _____ PM	☐ _____ PM
Other:	Other:

General Observation Notes:

_____
_____
_____
_____
_____

Freshwater Fish Tank Log Book

Maintenance Parameters
Date: / /

Temperature:	% Water Change:
pH Levels:	Ammonia Levels:
Nitrite Levels:	Nitrate Levels:
Alkalinity Levels:	Salinity Levels:
Phosphate Levels:	Added Water Conditioner: Y or N
Lights Schedule Time	**Feeding Schedule Times**
ON _____ AM	☐ _____ AM
OFF _____ PM	☐ _____ PM
Other:	Other:

General Observation Notes:

_____

_____

_____

_____

_____

Freshwater Fish Tank Log Book

Maintenance Parameters
Date: / /

Temperature:	% Water Change:
pH Levels:	Ammonia Levels:
Nitrite Levels:	Nitrate Levels:
Alkalinity Levels:	Salinity Levels:
Phosphate Levels:	Added Water Conditioner: Y or N
Lights Schedule Time	**Feeding Schedule Times**
ON _____ AM	☐ _____ AM
OFF _____ PM	☐ _____ PM
Other:	Other:

General Observation Notes:

_____

_____

_____

_____

_____

Freshwater Fish Tank Log Book

Maintenance Parameters
Date: / /

Temperature:	% Water Change:
pH Levels:	Ammonia Levels:
Nitrite Levels:	Nitrate Levels:
Alkalinity Levels:	Salinity Levels:
Phosphate Levels:	Added Water Conditioner: Y or N
Lights Schedule Time	**Feeding Schedule Times**
ON _____ AM	☐ _____ AM
OFF _____ PM	☐ _____ PM
Other:	Other:

General Observation Notes:

_____

_____

_____

_____

_____

Freshwater Fish Tank Log Book

Maintenance Parameters
Date: / /

Temperature:	% Water Change:
pH Levels:	Ammonia Levels:
Nitrite Levels:	Nitrate Levels:
Alkalinity Levels:	Salinity Levels:
Phosphate Levels:	Added Water Conditioner: Y or N
Lights Schedule Time	**Feeding Schedule Times**
ON _____ AM	☐ _____ AM
OFF _____ PM	☐ _____ PM
Other:	Other:

General Observation Notes:

_____

_____

_____

_____

_____

Freshwater Fish Tank Log Book

Maintenance Parameters
Date: / /

Temperature:	% Water Change:
pH Levels:	Ammonia Levels:
Nitrite Levels:	Nitrate Levels:
Alkalinity Levels:	Salinity Levels:
Phosphate Levels:	Added Water Conditioner: Y or N
Lights Schedule Time	**Feeding Schedule Times**
ON _____ AM	☐ _____ AM
OFF _____ PM	☐ _____ PM
Other:	Other:

General Observation Notes:

_____
_____
_____
_____
_____
_____

Freshwater Fish Tank Log Book

Maintenance Parameters
Date: / /

Temperature:	% Water Change:
pH Levels:	Ammonia Levels:
Nitrite Levels:	Nitrate Levels:
Alkalinity Levels:	Salinity Levels:
Phosphate Levels:	Added Water Conditioner: Y or N
Lights Schedule Time	**Feeding Schedule Times**
ON _____ AM	☐ _____ AM
OFF _____ PM	☐ _____ PM
Other:	Other:

General Observation Notes:

_____
_____
_____
_____
_____

Freshwater Fish Tank Log Book

Maintenance Parameters
Date: / /

Temperature:	% Water Change:
pH Levels:	Ammonia Levels:
Nitrite Levels:	Nitrate Levels:
Alkalinity Levels:	Salinity Levels:
Phosphate Levels:	Added Water Conditioner: Y or N
Lights Schedule Time	**Feeding Schedule Times**
ON _____ AM	☐ _____ AM
OFF _____ PM	☐ _____ PM
Other:	Other:

General Observation Notes:

_____
_____
_____
_____
_____
_____

Freshwater Fish Tank Log Book

Maintenance Parameters
Date: / /

Temperature:	% Water Change:
pH Levels:	Ammonia Levels:
Nitrite Levels:	Nitrate Levels:
Alkalinity Levels:	Salinity Levels:
Phosphate Levels:	Added Water Conditioner: Y or N
Lights Schedule Time	**Feeding Schedule Times**
ON _____ AM	☐ _____ AM
OFF _____ PM	☐ _____ PM
Other:	Other:

General Observation Notes:

_____

_____

_____

_____

Freshwater Fish Tank Log Book

Maintenance Parameters Date: / /	
Temperature:	% Water Change:
pH Levels:	Ammonia Levels:
Nitrite Levels:	Nitrate Levels:
Alkalinity Levels:	Salinity Levels:
Phosphate Levels:	Added Water Conditioner: Y or N
Lights Schedule Time	**Feeding Schedule Times**
ON _____ AM	☐ _____ AM
OFF _____ PM	☐ _____ PM
Other:	Other:

General Observation Notes:

_____
_____
_____
_____
_____
_____

Freshwater Fish Tank Log Book

Maintenance Parameters
Date: / /

Temperature:	% Water Change:
pH Levels:	Ammonia Levels:
Nitrite Levels:	Nitrate Levels:
Alkalinity Levels:	Salinity Levels:
Phosphate Levels:	Added Water Conditioner: Y or N
Lights Schedule Time	**Feeding Schedule Times**
ON _____ AM	☐ _____ AM
OFF _____ PM	☐ _____ PM
Other:	Other:

General Observation Notes:
_____
_____
_____
_____
_____

Freshwater Fish Tank Log Book

Maintenance Parameters
Date: / /

Temperature:	% Water Change:
pH Levels:	Ammonia Levels:
Nitrite Levels:	Nitrate Levels:
Alkalinity Levels:	Salinity Levels:
Phosphate Levels:	Added Water Conditioner: Y or N
Lights Schedule Time	**Feeding Schedule Times**
ON _____ AM	☐ _____ AM
OFF _____ PM	☐ _____ PM
Other:	Other:

General Observation Notes:

_____

_____

_____

_____

_____

www.ingramcontent.com/pod-product-compliance
Lightning Source LLC
Chambersburg PA
CBHW062240240225
22507CB00007B/475